Txtversations

How Old Farts <u>Must</u> Communicate With
Young Whipper-Snappers
More Effectively,
And Vice Versa
(So We Can Get On With Life &
Get Things Accomplished)

Sylvia Henderson

Txtversations: How Old Farts Must Communicate With Young
Whipper-Snappers More Effectively, and Vice Versa

(So We Can Get On With Life & Get Things Accomplished)

Published by:
V-Twin Press
P.O. Box 588
Olney, MD 20830-0588
USA

All rights reserved. No part of this book may be reproduced or transmitted in any form or by any means, electronic or mechanical, including photocopying, recording or by any information storage and retrieval method without written permission from the author, except for the inclusion of brief quotations in a review.

Permission inquiries should be addressed to the publisher.

Copyright © 2010 by Sylvia Henderson.

Printed in the United States of America

Includes reference notes and graphics.
ISBN# 978-1-932197-31-0

E-book version available at http://www.SpringboardTraining.com

Txtversations

© Sylvia Henderson

CEO, Springboard Training

Txtversation (n.): Communications between two or more people via short text messages (fewer than about 150 characters) using such means as SMS text messages, Twitter, instant messaging, e-mail, online message boards, or machine conversion of voicemail to text.

Txtversations may use emoticons and abbreviations typical of texting; standard English with spelled-out words and full sentences; or any combination. Txtversational skills are increasingly important for being understood and for avoiding misunderstandings.

Also spelled "textversation". First known use: August 20th, 2006, by a blogger known only as kateirule. (You do, Kate).

Txtversations: How Old Farts Must Communicate With Young Whipper-Snappers …

...More Effectively, & Vice Versa (So We Can Get On With Life & Get Things Accomplished)

Acknowledgements

Many thanks to Bud Smith for his invaluable help with the technicalities, norms, and details involved in research for this book.

Dedication

This book is dedicated to all us old farts (and I include myself in this category) for whom texting is an unnatural act, and to all you young whipper-snappers to whom we leave the workplace (and our futures) in capable and well-exercised thumbs.

Txtversations: How Old Farts <u>Must</u> Communicate With Young Whipper-Snappers ...

Foreword

Text messaging. Does it come naturally to you as a communications tool?

If your answer is "yes", then this book is for you because in it you will find:
- How to communicate more effectively with those for whom texting is an unnatural act.
- Why doing so is important to your professional success.
- When texting is, perhaps, not the best communications choice to make for your message.
- Some interesting "how we came to be where we now are" facts.

If your answer is "no", then this book is for you because in it you will find:
- How to communicate more effectively with those for whom texting is a way of life.
- Why doing so is important to your professional success.
- When texting is, perhaps, the best communications choice to make for your message.
- How to interpret text message codes.
- Text messaging etiquette tips.
- Some interesting "how we came to be where we now are" facts.

The benefit for you whether you answered "yes" or "no"? This book helps you to communicate more effectively, thereby positioning you for greater professional and personal success.

Thumbs up! And let's get to having more effective textversations.

Txtversations: How Old Farts <u>Must</u> Communicate With Young Whipper-Snappers ...

Table of Contents

Introduction   11
   How Did We Get Here? (Texting)
   Why is Texting Popular?
   A Little Birdie Told Me! Or, The Ascent of Twitter™
   Txtversations

Chapter 1. The Joy of Txt   25
   Communications Theory and Texting
   Historical Examples
   Text Messaging History
   Text Messaging in the News

Chapter 2. When to Txt   39
   Texting Across Platforms - Plusses
   Texting Across Platforms - Minuses
   So, When to Text?
   And, When Not to Text?

Chapter 3. Types of Txt   47
   SMS Text Messages
   Instant Messages
   Tweeting on Twitter™
   Text-Style Email and More

Chapter 4. Better Txt   57
   Text Message Marketing
   Text-Speak and Text Message Abbreviations
   Emoticons

Chapter 5. Txt Mastery   69
   Fixing Common Texting Errors
   Whom You Text

Why You Text
When You Text
When To Avoid Texting

Chapter 6. Txtversations   **79**
Txtversational Green, Yellow, and Red Light Zones
Your Txtversational Style
So What? Now What?

About the Author   **95**

Introduction

Texting is all over the news, and is part of mainstream culture. Text messages have helped elect a US President - and helped get sports stars, celebrities, and ordinary people in big trouble.

Those of us who are less experienced with texting - mostly, but not all, born prior to 1980 - are a bit confused by it all. Do I have to text? When? Should I misspell? Curse? Or just be myself?

And those of you who are more experienced with texting - mostly, but not all, born from 1980 onward - have trouble understanding why anyone could be confused. Why do they leave me stupid voice mail messages, instead of texting me? When should I text them? Do I have to spell correctly? Stop cursing? Or just be myself?

The answer to the last question is, unfortunately, "no" - for both groups. Don't just be yourself, disregarding who is on the other end of the message. Communication is shared between people. To be effective, it has to be understandable, and comfortable, for both parties. Both parties share in this responsibility.

More generally, the answer to these questions is the same for effective texting as it is for so much else in life: Knowledge is power. You only need to know a little bit, learn a little bit, and think just a little bit before acting, to use texting much more effectively. Text-like communications have been around, in one form or another, for centuries. Their current explosion into almost everyone's life, as an expected form of communication and social currency, isn't really that hard to get used to.

The telegraph, using Morse code, introduced an early form of texting. Yet the emergence of brief messages sent using just letters, numbers and punctuation - texts - has been a complete surprise. As communications tools got more powerful - think of the "land line" telephone, cell phones, and computers - the predominant trend was toward more natural and realistic communications, not brief, text-only ones. How did texting become so important - and why?

This book is more than a dissertation on texting. As an expert on interpersonal communications competencies, I encounter two types of people in the world today: (1) those for whom texting is a "natural act" and a comfortable form of communication, and (2) those for whom texting is a foreign language, and who wonder what happened to the written language "as we knew it"?

I write this book to serve as a help manual for both types of people. For those who are texting experts and have well-developed thumb muscles, this book will help you to communicate with people for whom full sentences and pen-and-paper are still preferred means of communication. More than that, in the business and professional world, solid communications skills are a necessity, and it IS possible to appropriately integrate your texting skills and habits into your professional modus operandi. This book helps you to bring these skills together.

For those who avoid texting like the plague and think it is an alien act performed by people who communicate on a different frequency, this book will help you to open your mind (I hope) to texting as a valid communications medium; to become more comfortable with the process; and to practice newly-acquired skills. You will better be able to communicate with those who are part of an emerging workforce and social transformation, and make positive strides towards understanding what may be an unfamiliar communications model.

How Did We Get Here? (Texting)

The "how" part was almost an accident. Text messaging was added to mobile phones as a kind of basic communication when a phone conversation might not be possible. It was available on most mobile phones as usage grew - slowly in the early 1990s, more rapidly in the later 1990s, and into a multi-billion-customer proposition into the 2000s.

The original limitation of text messages to roughly 160 characters was chosen almost randomly. It means that text messages impose a very light burden on cellular networks in terms of data transfer.

The 160-character limit, though, has practically gone by the wayside in current use. Twitter reduced message lengths to 140 characters. (More on Twitter.com later.)

People tend to send text messages that are short or very short. A full, properly punctuated English sentence is considered a very long text message by many. Telephone texting plans charge for more than one text message after 160 characters. It is frustrating, when texting, to find that the next communication needs to be long, often leading to a switch to a voice call or sending an e-mail.

Text messaging was originally used popularly by teenagers because it was cheap. This might seem less of a worry today, with inclusive cell phone calling and data plans, but anyone who has had a several-hundred-dollar bill for phone service, or Internet service in the days of metered access, realizes it is not a trivial concern.

Teenagers, being creative - and perhaps attempting to keep conversations from being understood by adults - developed a new form of communication known as "textspeak" (or "txtspk" for short). Textspeak uses extreme abbreviations, minimal capitalization and punctuation - "howru" for "How are you?" - and emoticons, icons created from keyboard characters to express emotions. The most popular emoticon is the infamous smiley face :), but there are many others; see Chapter 3.

A different form of text messaging became popular on computers. Known as instant messaging, it also offered instant, short, textual interactions between people. Like text messaging on phones, instant messaging was popular with teenagers, who seemed to have the dexterity required, and to juggle the interruptions involved better than older people.

As mobile phone usage exploded, and as mobile phones became ever-present, personal, seemingly private tools - more on that later – it is text messaging that has most captured people's attention and garnered more usage.

At the same time, text messaging has become a style of communications that is independent of its medium. Even when richer forms of communication are possible on a given communications platform, people continue to use the brevity of text messaging. People use text messaging-style communication and emoticons in email, online message boards, handwritten notes and other forms of communication. The noise and interruptions inherent in mobile phone conversations tend to push them to shorter, simpler, and fewer statements before reaching an end.

The name for one of the technical underpinnings of texting on mobile phones - SMS, or Short Message Service - sums up what is going on. People tend to think of one another as providing services - information, affirmation, even affection - that are often best elicited and provided by short messages.

Today, textspeak even affects f2f - textspeak for "face to face" - conversations. Formerly common expressions like "as I was saying" – AIWS, or "on the other hand" - OTOH in textspeak, as well as body language such as taking a deep breath before speaking, are met with impatience or even incredulity by listeners running at a faster pace. People are increasingly asked, or told, to be brief.

Emergency networks allow text communications when cellular networks are overloaded, as was made evident during the early hours of the 9/11 terrorist attacks on New York City and Washington DC, as well as subsequent natural and human-caused disasters of the early 21st century.

What Is "SMS"?

Wikipedia defines SMS as follows: "Short Message Service (SMS) is a communication service component of the GSM mobile communication system, using standardized communications protocols that allow the exchange of short text messages between mobile phone devices. SMS text messaging is the most widely used data application in the world, with 2.4 billion active users, or 74% of all mobile phone subscribers. Because of its ubiquity, the term SMS is used as a synonym for all types of short text messaging, as well as the user activity itself, in many parts of the world."

See http://en.wikipedia.org/wiki/SMS for more.

Why is Texting Popular?

At one time, our visions of future communications were well represented by the Dick Tracy wrist phone, with live video keeping "coppers" in touch. Yet, at a time when such videophones are possible, we spend more and more time sending messages using only text. Why is texting so popular?

Texting has many advantages - and is just plain fun to boot. Let's begin, though, with a look at some of the disadvantages of texting, to help us understand and appreciate how to use texting better - and when, perhaps, not to use it. Here are the main problems with texting (see if you can think of any others):

- **Hard to do**. Adults in particular often find texting difficult on a telephone keypad (press the 2 key twice for a "b", the 7 key four times for an "s", etc.) It's not easy even on a BlackBerry™-style full keyboard. We adults tend to find texting a pain in the, well, s.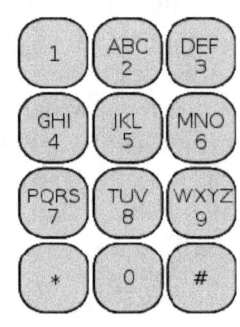

- **Low-bandwidth**, in communications terms; just words, and even a limited number of those. No tone of voice, no facial expressions, no body language - like email, only more so.

- **Dismissive**. Texts can easily feel dismissive, both in the tone (which tends to seem abrupt) and in the fact that someone couldn't be bothered to call. Being fired from a job, or dumped from a romantic relationship, by text is famous as a symbol of coldness and callousness. Of course, if that's the intention, this is an advantage, to the sender at least.

- **Expensive** (in aggregate). Texts are cheap individually, at about 20¢ each for an individual text message in the US, but expensive in aggregate, with heavy users sending perhaps hundreds of texts a day. If texts go beyond the number covered by a calling plan, an exchange of texts can easily be more expensive than a phone conversation covering the same ground.
- **Injurious**. Texting is hard on one's wrists and fingers. Many people have joked about the BlackBerry causing their thumbs to go numb, and there have been more serious problems with repetitive stress injuries (RSI) as well.
- **Discoverable**. Every text you send is recorded on your cell phone bill. Worse, unlike phone calls, unless you guard your phone very carefully, a jealous or curious friend or romantic partner can easily find the specifics of past texts. This can lead to personal relationship issues, or worse. Your workplace also has a record of your texts if you use a work-issued device for texting, or if you file your cell phone bill as part of an expense report.

So, if we were being harsh, we could describe texting as difficult, cold, expensive, and painful. How on Earth has it ever become so popular?

Looking back at its beginnings, texting first caught on with teenagers. There are some crucial good points about texting that particularly resonate with teenagers - which are also things that those who want to communicate with those who grew up texting should be aware of.

Here are the positive points of texting for those who grow up with "thumbs on keypads"; people for whom texting is a natural act:

- **New**. Teenagers love things that are new, which helped launch texting in the early days. With texting, not every teen had a cell phone, nor could all afford to send very many texts. Those who could, did.

- **Cheap** (individually). Sending a single text is about 20¢, much less than a typical phone call made outside a calling plan. Teenagers are being sensible when they send a text rather than making a call - but perhaps a bit unaware of how an exchange of messages can rack up the charges into a big overall bill.

- **Easy to do** (for teens). The same motions for generating characters that adults find difficult are easy for teens. I've seen teenagers text so fast that smoke seems to rise from the keypads of their phones. Laughing at the clumsiness adults demonstrate when trying to text is part of the fun too.

- **Highly context-specific**, in communications terms. That is, the limited bandwidth of texts means they are highly dependent on the shared experience of the sender and receiver - something interesting that happened in class that day, or something funny that was said on a favorite TV show, as well as the content of all the previous texts between the sender and the receiver.

- **New rules**. The physical difficulty of texting encourages a private language with shortened spellings (such as dropping vowels out of words) and abbreviations (LOL for Laughing Out Loud, ROTFL for Rolling On The Floor Laughing).

- **Less interruptive**. A text message is much less interruptive than a phone call. A text does not make the phone keep ringing until you answer it. You can quickly peek at a text even while talking to someone in person, and can be fully engaged in multiple txtversations while watching TV, listening to music, doing homework - or all at once.
- **Personal**. Done right, texting can feel very personal and intimate. It's just between two people, and again relies a lot on their shared context.
- **Private**. Teenagers are often limited in their ability to have privacy. As long as they can trust their parents and siblings - or as long as they lock their phones with a password - they can keep the contents private.

So we can understand how texting took off for teenagers. It was new, different, and distinctive - you stood out if you had a cell phone, more so if you could afford to use it. Many of the negatives for adults, such as the sheer difficulty, were less of a problem or even a positive for teens.

That all makes sense, but how did texting stay with teens as they became adults - and even become popular with older adults who had never developed the habit when they were young? Some technological changes contributed to texting and enabled the medium to grow in popularity:

- **Better phone keyboards (1)**. It took the BlackBerry and its always-available physical keyboard to make texting and e-mailing - usually with short messages - popular among adults.

- **Better phone keyboards (2).** The wildly popular iPhone also has a full keyboard, though it is a "soft" keyboard, made available by software, requiring the user to type on glass. It's easy enough for adults to manage it, but hard enough to discourage long messages (and to encourage text-style abbreviations and carelessness about minor misspellings).

- **Inclusive texting plans.** Adults hate managing one-off expenses like a dime or two each for texts. Inclusive texting plans encourage an "all you can text" approach. (Ironically, many adults would be better off paying separately for each individual text, as they do not do it that much.)

- **Coolness factor.** As teenagers grew up, and a few "early adopter" older adults started texting, it became uncool not to text - and if your boss texts you, or even your child, you have to respond. So it became more or less necessary for adults to learn.

- **Moving to the computer.** Adults tend to like the larger screens and expansive, physical keyboards of a computer much more than the tiny ones on portable devices - though a BlackBerry™ (or similar device) is a well-designed compromise. As texting from the computer has become easier, and alternatives have arisen such as short emails across platforms, texting has grown more popular with adults.

Even with all this analysis, the sheer popularity of texting, textspeak, and txtversations is still a bit of a mystery and phenomenon. It might even have turned out that text-style communications might have eventually become less popular - until the rise of another texting-style communications medium came along and took texting to new heights.

A Little Birdie Told Me! Or, The Ascent of Twitter™

Texting was already a communications method of steadily increasing importance when a new communications tool emerged with even greater effect on how we communicate, and on our culture as a whole.

Twitter™ (Twitter.com) was created by Jack Dorsey and introduced in 2006. It is based on tweets, text-based posts of up to 140 characters. These are expressly based on SMS messages, with their 160-character limit.

Twitter can be linked to Web sites and other Internet addresses, and tweets can thereby be used to link to photos, videos, music and other media files. Internet addresses (URLs) are shortened to approximately 12-15 characters using services such as bit.ly and tinyurl. The use of multimedia is only by reference links; the messages themselves, called "tweets", are still text-only, and must fall within the 140-character limit.

Twitter has millions of users. It is heavily used by journalists, politicians, bloggers, certain celebrities, and others for whom being up-to-date and staying connected is at an absolute premium.

Twitter was used to send the first news and photographs of the landing of US Airways Flight 1549 on the Hudson River in mid-January, 2009. This was one of the first times that Twitter users were the first to report breaking mainstream news and, for a brief but crucial period, the only medium to be up-to-date on a story that the world wanted to know about. The successful river landing of Flight 1549 and the rescue of all its passengers was an incredible, heroic, nearly miraculous event that was first made known to the world through Twitter.

Later in the same year, Twitter was used by Iranians protesting their country's elections. Tweets evaded censors and kept people around the world, including the large Iranian diaspora, involved in real time updates as startling scenes unfolded on the streets of Tehran and other Iranian cities.

Twitter played a major role in the communications that facilitated the election of the first African-American President of the United States, Barack Obama. Word of entertainment icon Michael Jackson's death spread within minutes, literally, across the world due to the tool.

Twitter has created a number of stars, dethroned others, and enhanced the impact of people who were already more or less well known through other media. Journalists such as David Pogue, the technology columnist for the New York Times, have become even better known through their frequent - one might sometimes say relentless - tweeting. Those who tweet in ways that seem rote or insincere on the one hand, or overly personal or even obscene on the other, quickly find their audience declining - on Twitter, and perhaps in other media as well.

Txtversations

Twitter makes excruciatingly clear what was already evident in the use of textspeak for text messages, instant messaging, and in other media: not only are the individual messages, or texts, important. Also important are the overall conversations and their effect on the parties involved.

I call these complete two-way communications exchanges "txtversations". Dropping the initial "e" in "text" reminds us that txtversations take place in an abbreviated form. But the use of the whole word reminds us that the messages may be just dots of paint on a canvas; only the accumulation of dots in specific patterns produce a picture.

> "I submit that text messaging, and the management of the overall txtversations that result, is an emerging and indispensable new skill."
>
> – *Sylvia Henderson, Interpersonal Skills Expert*

Those of us who communicate as an important part of our work and personal lives - which means most of us, if not just about everyone - need to master a few keystroke skills to thrive. I submit that text messaging, and the management of the overall txtversations that result, is an emerging and indispensable new skill.

You can use txtversations to "build your brand" - to become better-known and better-respected. And you can avoid, or quickly recover from, crucial mistakes that could otherwise lead to a sudden drop in popularity and impact.

To increase your txtversational impact requires knowledge and skill. I seek to impart the requisite building blocks of knowledge, and to enhance the required skills, in the coming pages.

Chapter 1. The Joy of Txt

We have been motivated to communicate who we are, what we do, how we feel, what we need, our philosophies, beliefs, and cultural norms throughout history. We purportedly have the most advanced language skills of any species, and are the only known species to transmit and preserve what is usually said in words via writing.

Texting is a natural outgrowth of different kinds of communications techniques that people have used throughout history. However, past systems using brief messages were driven by absolute necessity. When people used smoke signals, or semaphore flags, or Morse code to send and receive messages, brevity was enforced by the medium.

What is fascinating about texting is how quickly and energetically people rush to use the medium, even when alternatives - seemingly similar or better in price, convenience, and richness - are available.

Even though text messages have a fixed, 160-character limit, that is not really what drives most texts, as they are commonly far under the character limit. We must just really love to text.

Communications Theory and Texting

Communications theory can be used to break down each communication between two parties into four elements: a sender, a receiver, a message, and a context. Let's look at

how these elements interact in texting and similar means of communication:

- **Sender**. The sender decides to communicate and to use text messaging as the means by which to communicate.
- **Receiver**. The receiver finds it difficult to truly ignore a text message unless his or her device is turned off. The receiver may "ignore" the message in a social sense - not act on it nor reply to it - but the message itself is hard to miss.
- **Message**. This is one of the simplest communications structures that can be considered theoretically: 160 characters of text, including letters, numbers, and special characters.
- **Context**. This is all-important to <u>understanding</u> the communicated message. The sender and receiver must speak the same language, both literally - or the message won't be understood - and figuratively, in that texts often refer to a great deal of contextual information. "Dlt slide 4 fm 2day's preso" (delete slide #4 from today's presentation) hardly means anything except between two people who know each other and are referring to a very 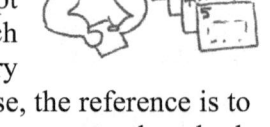 specific situation. Indeed, in this case, the reference is to a specific presentation file whose contents they both know well.

In considering txtversations - extended interactions where much or all of the communication is via text - we focus on how to get the specific communications (specific text messages) and timing right. However, we also need to keep in mind the choices available to the sender and the receiver, and the context in which the interaction occurs.

Historical Examples

A brief look at the history of text-type communications helps us consider the elements of text communications in a broad context. We can better appreciate the opportunities we have in texting when we see the roles of other short-exchange communications in our history.

American Sign Language

American Sign Language - widely known as ASL and also as Ameslan - is a world standard for communications among people with severe hearing challenges, even those for whom English, and in particular American English, is not their native language. It is often used in combination with gestures and, to some degree, with reading lip movements or facial expressions. Meaning is heavily dependent on the context in which the communication is taking place.

ASL was devised in 1815 when a minister, Thomas Hopkins Gallaudet, visited Europe on a quest to find methods for teaching the deaf. He went to Paris and studied the methods of the French Royal Institution for the Deaf. Returning to the US with a student from the Royal Institution, he founded the Connecticut Asylum for the Education and Instruction of Deaf and Dumb Persons, now called the American School for the Deaf, still based in Connecticut. While the practice of sending children with hearing impairments away to separate schools has become less prevalent, the American School for the Deaf continues in operation today.

ASL is a separate language that only partially depends on finger spelling. Finger spelling is sign language at its most basic: individual hand gestures replace individual letters. Even among people who use finger spelling, certain words have their own gestures, which may be a mashup of the finger symbols used to spell the word out letter by letter, or unique symbols with their own derivation and history.

There are also many symbols and gestures unique to ASL, as well as dialects, both in America and among the many users of ASL in other countries. The same is true of texting.

Underground Railroad Quilt Code

Slave quilt messages are a fascinating form of short-message communication. Under laws in force in the American South under slavery (from before the founding of the USA up through the end of the Civil War in 1865), it was illegal to teach slaves to read and write. It was also illegal to help them escape, though the status of such laws in the North was a matter of intense debate, and even a cause of riots and other disruptions.

Quilt patterns were used by African-American slaves to record their history and pass it down through the generations. The underground railroad quilt code was used more specifically to help slaves escape to freedom in the North and Canada. Patterns in quilts symbolized directions, safe passage conditions, sympathetic households, and other travel messages. The patterns and their symbolism comprised abbreviated messages understood by those who "spoke the same language" and could interpret the messages conveyed. This is one of the major components of communicating effectively – understanding the language being used to communicate, and its nuances. Thus, quilt codes could be considered a rudimentary – yet elaborate – form of text messaging.

(Interpretations of the use of quilt patterns in the Underground Railroad is controversial, as, by their nature, there are few written records of them. Most of what is known has been passed down through oral history. However, African-American oral history has proven reliable as a source of information in other instances, and we therefore trust it here.)

Some of the patterns used in these quilts included:

- Flying geese. A reminder that in the spring, when most slaves escaped, geese were migrating north. They not only indicated the direction, but led the way to watering holes and resting spots.
- North Star. A reminder to follow the North Star, also a signal that an opportunity was upcoming.
- Crossroads. A symbol referring to Cleveland, Ohio, a crossroads with several routes to freedom on the Underground Railroad.
- Drunkard's path. Turn south for some period, or more generally, follow a weaving, wavering path to throw off pursuers.
- Shoofly. A symbol representing a person who could guide or help the slave.
- Log Cabin. A symbol indicating a safe house.

Morse Code and Tap Codes

In the early 1840s, Samuel Morse had a problem. He invented a new communications device - the telegraph - and needed a language to use with it. So he invented the language that became known as Morse code. Just like a modern entrepreneur, he had to invent software to make his hardware work.

The telegraph transmits a buzzing sound when a key is depressed. The key tap is a binary code - sound is either not being transmitted, or it is. No reliable modulation of the sounds themselves was possible, just "off" and "on".

Morse code was designed to work within this "on / off" limitation in the most efficient manner possible. It was based on two different symbols, short and long sounds. The "off" sound was only a separator between the short and long sounds.

In the hands of an experienced telegraph operator - and an equally experienced receiver and transcriber - the short sounds could be very short indeed, the long sounds only a tiny bit longer, and the gaps between them very short as well. A commonly used marker such as STOP - which marked the end of a sentence - might be shortened to the point of being unrecognized by any but the most skilled interpreter.

Skilled operators could understand Morse code at a rate of about 40 words per minute, whereas a skilled typist using a keyboard might reach 60 words per minute. (Perhaps a skilled user of a telephone-style keypad can reach 40 words per minute while texting.) The use of Morse code tended to avoid shortenings of words or the use of most acronyms due to the possibility of misinterpretation.

A considerable amount of interpretation might be needed to accurately receive and transcribe a message, especially one where similar words occurred near to each other or that had a great deal of unfamiliar content. Jokes about mistaken telegraph messages were common during the time that telegraph communications were common, which was right up to and through the Second World War. The symbol SOS, made up of the codes for each of the letters - three dots, three dashes, and three dots again - is still widely used today.

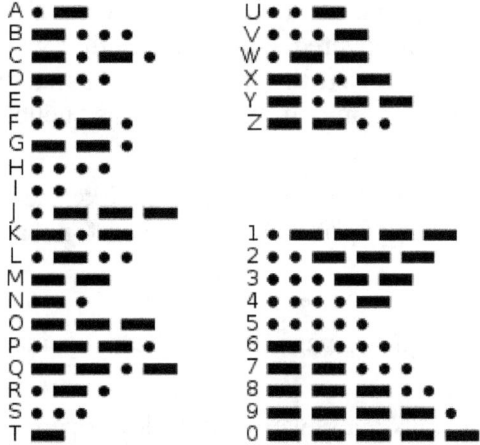

International Morse Code Symbols

Text Messaging History

The earliest text messages similar to what we use today and discuss in this book were transmitted using pagers, beginning approximately in 1989. Early pagers could only send the numeric digits 0 through 9, as well as a dash, in order to transmit the phone number the recipient was then supposed to call. People discovered that many digits, when read upside-down, can be viewed as letters - a "4" as an "h", a "3" as an "E" - and some common words, such as "hello", were sent this way.

This kind of number/text code looks like the following string of numbers, read upside-down and therefore backwards:

$$01134$$

Go ahead. Turn this page, or your head, upside down to see for yourself!

True text messages were first developed as a means of communication for the hearing impaired via the TTY, or Text Telephone, system. TTY communications are much like text messaging, but used over normal phone lines. Laws in various countries have long required that telephone service providers include some form of text transmission for people with hearing challenges, and mobiles were no exception. Text messaging was integrated from earlier days.

The first public use of text messaging was in a commercial to promote the Vodafone mobile phone network in the UK in 1992. The message was sent from a desktop computer. The message was simple: "Merry Christmas".

Text messaging grew slowly until it became popular among teenagers in the 1990's, and gradually grew to encompass more and more people. There are several billion (!) mobile phones in use worldwide today, and an estimated 80% of users send and receive text messages fairly regularly.

For various reasons, text messaging was slower to catch on in the US than in Europe and other countries, and slower to grow beyond the initial teenage population as well. Text message use is approximately 20% less in the US than elsewhere, even today, at least as of this writing.

Mention of text messaging in the media is common worldwide. Mentions were few and far between during the 1990s, but skyrocketed in the year 2000, reaching perhaps 10 times their earlier number. They have continued fairly steadily ever since, at a very high level - indicating the acceptance of texting as a mainstream form of communication. Increasingly, major media outlets report more and more on text messaging as a phenomenon and as a growing mainstream tool.

Text Messaging in the News

The following are some representative mentions of text messaging in the news. These excerpts show the variety of instances in which texting comes up as a news-worthy topic.

- New York Newsday, September 30, 1993. "Users of NeXT Computers can send voice and text messages only to each other." The NeXT Computer was Steve Jobs' pet project between leaving Apple in the late 1980s and returning triumphantly in the late 1990s, after Apple bought Next. (He had another project at the same time, Pixar, which became a multi-billion-dollar success with the movie *Toy Story* and was bought out by Walt Disney.) This story reminds us that text messaging between different technology platforms was a long time coming.
- Los Angeles Times, April 27, 1994. "Some paging companies provide software to let personal computers and Macs send text messages-rather than simply a phone number-to their alphanumeric pagers." This seems to signal the beginning of widespread use of text messaging in the form in which we know it today. The primary difference is that pagers were receive-only devices enabling one-way-only communications (from a sender to the receiver in possession of the pager).
- Seattle Post-Intelligencer, Feb 27, 1996. "The promotion urged customers to vote via text messages for their favorite ... Some 30 percent of those sending text messages had never done so before." Text messaging is

catching on, with companies using it for promotions. More and more new users try texting for the first time.

- USA TODAY, Aug 25, 1999. "Send text messages to other users instead of calling them. ... Kids have become so facile at creating text messages with a single thumb punching a phone." Early recognition at the prevalence of texting among teenagers. (A bit insulting to call them "kids", which to a teenager is anyone 12 or under; at that time, few kids, narrowly defined, had mobile phones.)

- UK Telegraph, May 24, 2001: "Children sending text messages on mobile phones in the playground could be risking their health, according to doctors who...". There goes the press with "children" again! I'm almost starting to feel sorry for teenagers. This is an early recognition of health problems due to texting; note that it's not mentioned as a problem for adults.

- BBC News, March 25, 2002. "Ever "lost" a text message? Ever claimed not to have received one when you did? The fact is, text messages go missing." Now text messaging is starting to get traction with adults, at least in the UK - because what adult writer would bother to pen a newspaper article if it was only "kids" who were suffering?

- New York Times, July 3, 2004. "China has begun filtering billions of telephone text messages to ensure that people do not use the popular communication tool to undermine...". More evidence of adult use - the content of text messages is now important enough to censor.

- MSNBC.com, December 5, 2006. "Technology, some lucky text messages and an outdoorsman's intuition helped locate three members of a family stranded in the Oregon...". Text messaging has become so mainstream, even in the US, that it helps out in an emergency.
- The Detroit News, December 14, 2009. "The Supreme Court is expected to decide as soon as Monday whether to hear an appeal of a case in which employees won a constitutional right to privacy in their text messages..." Ownership and access to text messages continues to make news.

Text messages have repeatedly proven their ability to get through from sender to receiver when other messages cannot, in ways that have also made news. Passengers in the planes hijacked during the tragic 9/11 attacks in 2001 used a combination of phone calls and text messages to communicate with those on the ground. Some people trapped in the World Trade Center towers were also able to send poignant final text messages before the buildings collapsed.

A cell phone call requires a complex set of connections within the cell phone network via satellites and towers - a level of connection that is not always available on the ground, and often not available at all in the air. Text messages are much less demanding technically than phone calls, and can often get through when a voice connection cannot be made.

Until or unless air travel laws change, air travellers cannot use their cell phones when in flight. This is purportedly due to potential interference with the avionics and with air traffic control signals. However, experience in emergencies shows that it can work.

The crash of US Airways Flight 1549 in the Hudson River in 2009 was, of course, memorialized by text messages. Early news of the crash came from Twitter user Janis Krums of Sarasota, Florida, who was on a ferry in the Hudson that day. His tweet: "There's a plane in the Hudson. I'm on the ferry going to pick up the people. Crazy."

Krums' accompanying photo of the plane, afloat, with passengers standing on the wings, flashed around the world. Within half an hour, Krums was being interviewed live on MSNBC, and a few hours later it was confirmed that all passengers survived.

Txtversations: How Old Farts <u>Must</u> Communicate With Young Whipper-Snappers ...

Chapter 2. When to Txt

Many of us who are adults today, and have been for a while, face some uncertainty as to when to use text messaging - that is, when to start, or stay in, a txtversation. This determination can influence your odds of success in a text conversation.

Youth and adults for whom texting is a common practice also face the decision of when to use text messaging as a communications medium. There are times in which texting is less appropriate and less effective as a communications format.

In this chapter we tackle when texting is an appropriate and inappropriate choice.

Texting Across Platforms - Plusses

Texting, on any platform, has several plusses.

Plus: Messages are concise

Text messages are short and, if you write well, clear. This saves time and effort. The informality of texting also helps save time and effort, in that little thought or preparation is needed to instantly text a message "on the fly".

Plus: Messages are documented and referenced

People often complain about the difficulty of remembering an in-person or voice conversation, or the related difficulty of reconstructing some e-mail exchanges (i.e, when the subject line changes). E-mail also presents the "needle in a haystack" conundrum of finding key points in a torrent of words. Text message exchanges are easy to find and to scan for key points -

at least on most modern mobile phones and devices that group exchanges together.

Plus: Messages cut through the clutter

For users unfamiliar with texting, the assumption is that people do not get a lot of text messages. When such a person receives a text message, that message typically "cuts through the clutter" and gets special attention. (This does imply that the message should be worth it and that the receiver knows how to retrieve it.)

Plus: Messages are low-key

Despite the importance given to texting, a text message can, in a way, be low-key. It does not demand that someone break off a meeting or conversation. It is akin to sending a human messenger with a note in to someone in a meeting, but even lower-key. This can be very welcome by the recipient, who can pick up on a quick fact - "the client will be 30 minutes late" - with little interruption to what they are doing.

Plus: Messages are private

Text messages are relatively private - only someone who has physical access to your mobile phone is likely to see them. While it's possible to forward a text message, it's much less frequently done than with e-mail messages, which are often copied to everyone and their best friend. This allows the texter to be clear, even pointed, without worrying about the effect on a large audience.

Texting Across Platforms - Minuses

To counter the plusses, there are several minuses to text messaging as well - some just the flip side of the pluses:

Minus: Messages are one-to-one

Sending a message to several people at once has its advantages. If you need to reach multiple recipients, it's easier to send email. Sending a text to multiple recipients is not only difficult; it's subject to all sorts of confusion and cross-talk as responses come back, some of which might also need to be seen by multiple people.

Minus: Messages are perceived as curt

Communications theorist Marshall McLuhan once said, "The medium is the message". This famous saying applies to text messaging. Text messages are perceived as a curt, brusque, even disdainful form of communication by those who dislike the medium. It is much easier to imagine a boss texting subordinates than vice versa - and when people do text their boss, they make somewhat tortuous efforts to be polite.

Minus: Messages are simplistic

The very brevity of text messages is often a negative. Receiving a seemingly simple message, such as "how's it going?", during a meeting, may require a long response. The recipient is thus left to ignore the text; to give a partial or misleading answer - "fine" instead of "they rejected our offer, but countered with a year's supply of Spam and two polo ponies"; or to break off the meeting to reply.

Minus: Texts invite misteaks (just kidding)

Many people find it permissible to include mistakes in texts - but the recipients may have higher standards. It's also physically difficult to enter a perfect text message, not least because "helpful" word substitution programs on some phones change accurate typing into inaccurate replacements. ("UCLA" might become "you say".) We expect forgiveness - but should try not to give ourselves permission.

Minus: Poorly timed messages are unwelcome

People often feel they just have to be available for text messages, so they leave their phones on. They may turn off the ringer for phone calls, but keep their ears open for the tone, chime, or little "buzz" of vibration that signals a text. The same signal that's subtle during a business meeting is all too compelling when you're trying to get to sleep after a long airplane flight into an unaccustomed time zone.

Minus: Messages can become public

Messages are easily found on one's telephone or smart device by anyone with access to the device.

So, When to Text?

While we are aware of these plusses and minuses, seeing them listed seems a bit intimidating. (I found it to be so, just looking at the list after I wrote it!)

So when are some good times to use a text message - and, for longer exchanges, to start a txtversation? There's no "one size fits all" answer, but here are some hints:

- **For reassurance**. A text message with a quick, factual update can be a big plus. "Got to NYC fine", "Just sent the check", and "Your father will be @ the 5th st. entrance" are examples of good messages to send by text.
- **For specificity**. Specific information is often good to send by text. Some people get daily stock alerts by text; "Mocha-Cola closes up 3/4 at 19 7/8" is a good use of texting.
- **For immediacy**. Some companies use mass text messages to alert key employees to disasters, for instance, or earnings announcements. "Reminder: CEO update on new product @ 4PM EST", for example. (Hopefully not simultaneously a new product announcement AND a disaster!)
- **For informality**. Sending a message by text can convey a feeling of informality and friendliness among, for instance, work colleagues, an "us against them" feeling of solidarity. "Lunch @ sub shop 2day. Noon."
- **For intimacy**. Smart spouses and romantic partners use texts to cut through the clutter of each others' day with

brief messages that are sweet, supportive - or saucy, without obligating the other person to reply. "Thinking of you", "Will be home by 7" and "I'm wearing THAT dress!" are fun things to text to a partner.

And, When Not to Text?

It is easy to "get on a roll" with texting and to start to use it for a really large proportion of communications. It is easy, convenient, recordable, and all the other plusses we previously mentioned. However, there are definitely some good times to think twice before texting, such as the following:

- **Texting the boss**. This is fine when expected and when conveying specific information, but it is the rare boss who will appreciate "wazup?" or a similar informal message.
- **Arguing via text**. Avoid texting when you are angry, and texting about things about which you are angry. Text messages can already seem cold and peremptory; using text when you intend to sound that way just makes it worse.
- **Sexting**. Sending messages that go beyond mildly risqué, let alone sending highly personal photos, is just dumb. This stuff can live in cyberspace forever. Like posting party pictures on Facebook that you end up wishing would just disappear, sending all-too-personal texts is just silly. And dangerous.
- **If you are not sure of the receiver's circumstances**. If you do not know what the recipient is doing, what time zone they are in, or who they are with, not texting is often the better part of valor. If you wake them up, interrupt that disco party, or cut into that long-delayed

elegant dinner with Him or Her, you may wish you'd never pressed Send.

The converse to this is that these may be exactly the times to text rather than call on the phone. The recipient can control when he or she reads the message. If that elegant dinner is so special, the text-receiving device had better be off anyway!

When financial considerations are key. There is a financial consideration to texting. Messages that exceed 160 characters count as two (or more) messages by some telecommunications carriers. Be sure that the person to whom you text has an unlimited (or high volume) text messaging plan or they will be charged by their communications carrier per message. This is definitely not appreciated by the recipient when he or she does not initiate the message expense. This is also why the idea of text spam and advertising is anathema to people, regardless of their messaging plan.

Txtversations: How Old Farts <u>Must</u> Communicate With Young Whipper-Snappers ...

Chapter 3. Types of Txt

More and more often, text messaging is the method people choose to make a point. Many people like text messages and expect to receive information by text.

Once you know you want to send a text message, you then have to decide which texting platform might be best. The choices are more numerous than you might think, and include:

- An SMS text message sent from one mobile device to another
- Use of instant messenger from one computer to another
- Using Twitter
- Text-style email.

Let's take a look at each type of texting method so you can decide not just what to say, but with on which texting platform you will choose to say it.

SMS Text Messages

SMS text messages - "true" text messages - are the most popular form of texting and are what most people think of when they think of text messaging.

SMS text messages arrive at, and are sent from, a mobile phone - which many people carry at all times, and have nearby even when they are asleep. The decision whether to have it turned on, set to vibrate only, or turned off completely is a circumstantial one.

Coming from and going to the device that people keep closest to them, SMS text messages are most subject to both the positives and negatives of text messages:

+ Concise; cutting through the clutter; potentially being low-key; privacy.
− Potentially curt; simplistic; mistake-prone; potentially poorly timed.

SMS text messages also have a downside that is not as strong for most other forms of text messaging: they can't include Web links, and the recipient usually can't quickly go to a Web page for reference. They're isolated from a crucial source of information that people increasingly depend on.

Your ability to send an SMS text message is clearly limited to people whose mobile phone number you have. This may be only close friends, family members, and close co-workers and business colleagues.

Even if you have access to a wider range of mobile phone numbers - for instance, through a company phone list - think carefully before using them. We mostly expect to get text messages from a relatively small circle of people. If you're more or less a stranger to someone, consider using a different means of communication. If you do proceed, consider adopting a neutral tone - don't assume chumminess merely because you happen to have a person's cell phone number.

Also consider other media if you have needs that a text message might not fulfil. For instance, if other people really should see the message - or the response - consider using e-mail. Also consider e-mail if it's a long message - partly for your own ease of typing, partly for the recipient's ease of reading and dealing with the content.

If the back-and-forth is likely to be complicated, consider calling. You can use text messaging to arrange the call, in effect "warning" the person that a call is coming.

If the disadvantages are not show-stoppers, SMS text messages are usually the best way to take full advantage of texting as a communications medium.

Instant Messages

Instant messages, popularly known as IMs, are brief messages, usually text-only (but not exclusively). They are sent by friends, family members or colleagues - usually when both parties are using a computer and are online with an active Internet connection at the same time.

IMs are usually sent and received via computer, so their plusses and minuses are a bit different from an SMS text message. The sender has access to a physical QWERTY keyboard, which is also called a typewriter keyboard, and is the keyboard that comes with most desktop and mobile computers. IMs may not be as concise as text messages. There is, perhaps, less excuse for them to contain mistakes.

The timing issues in sending an IM are generally not as crucial as in sending a text, because the recipient is unlikely to have their computer on in such a way that an IM is going to interrupt a private conversation, or wake them up from a jet-lagged sleep.

There is a particular issue relating to IMs, timing, and privacy to watch out for. IMs often pop up on a computer screen rather suddenly - and a colleague may be looking at the screen at the time. Worse, the recipient may be giving a presentation. Many presenters have suddenly been left red-faced by a flirtatious or gossipy IM sent at a bad moment.

Our receptivity to IMs varies tremendously. Some people seem to feel they're barely alive if they aren't receiving a constant stream of SMS text messages, IMs, e-mails and so on. They may even heighten the chaos by listening to music, having the TV on, and more.

Others view IMs with anxiety and loathing. Their time and focus are precious, and they don't want to be interrupted unless it's really important.

Such a stance can be increasingly difficult to maintain. Some social circles seem to regard constant availability as a condition of membership. Some workplaces want you to be IM'ing away anytime you're at your desk, even if you're deep into your work.

It is not uncommon to be working on a carefully worded email to someone and receive an IM from them. Even long-established applications such as Lotus Notes™ - a corporate alternative to Microsoft Outlook™ and other personal information managers - have instant messaging capability.

Some of the readiness (or not) to engage in IM'ing has to do with a person's age. Some of it seems to track the introvert/extrovert axis. There is, however, another factor, relating to how people view technology.

Some people, seduced by the ever-growing capabilities of computers connected to ever-faster networks, seem to treat their computer as an environment, embodying work, personal business, and all else. Such people are almost always on their computers.

Others, perhaps put off by various physical aches and pains that computers can cause, are trying to take their life back from their computers. They treat them only as tools for work and personal business, but try to keep them shut off as much as possible.

Luckily, one of the best features of IM tools helps here. Most of them indicate whether the recipient is online and ready to receive messages. So you have at least a fighting chance of being able to adjust your desire to send an IM to the recipient's readiness to receive it.

Tweeting on Twitter™

Twitter is perhaps the most famous Internet service to emerge in the early 21st Century, though it has fewer users than a longer-established service like Facebook. Yet it has a big influence through the concentration of its users among journalists, highly technically oriented people, and certain celebrities and politicians.

If you use Twitter, you'll know it's a great tool for staying informed of key topics and about key people whose tweets you "follow". There is also a certain amount of cross-posting, via re-tweeting, of key messages from one group to another. Tweets also show up in blogs, or cause emails to be sent or even news stories to appear.

Beyond this cross-pollination, many tweets disappear into the ether, scarcely noted or acknowledged beyond a very small group, if at all.

I avoid creating a user manual for Twitter here, Yet I add a few notes to introduce Twitter to those of you who have not used it:

- To "be on Twitter" means that you went to the Twitter application (at Twitter.com) and registered yourself for a free account (free as of this writing, anyway). When you do so you create your own Twitter user identification. This allows you to send and receive tweets.

- "Tweets" are the text messages sent from one Twitter user to another. You can send and receive tweets by signing onto your Twitter account, or through many other applications available in the Web universe that have been created or modified to work with Twitter.
- "Tweeting" is the verb for sending and receiving such messages. When you learn of someone else who has a Twitter user identification (again, through a variety of ways beyond the scope of this book), and you want to connect with them, you "follow" them by selecting the "follow" function in Twitter. This is akin to "friending" or "connecting" with someone on other social media applications, or "bookmarking" a website you visit on your Internet browser.

That's it for my introduction to Twitter.

So how and when to use Twitter? You should use it when you have a message to send to people who you know follow you or the particular topic tags you add to your tweet. (This is a similar concept to adding keywords to articles and blog posts you may write for other Internet applications.) The tweet will definitely reach them.

While your message will technically reach your followers, they may not notice it. Most people who use Twitter are constantly besieged with tweets, and they have to shut off occasionally. Sometimes an important message gets thrown out along with the overall stream of tweets that threaten to inundate Twitter users.

It is difficult to respond directly to a tweet. While it is technically possible to send a private message, the capability is not all that heavily used. Avoid counting on immediate direct feedback that tells you that your message is getting across.

Consider a tweet a one-way, "broadcast" mode of communication. While you may receive a related response to your message, it is not the same kind of one-on-one communications that texting provides. Tweeting is like shouting a message across a public street. Maybe someone will shout back; maybe not. And the response could come from anyone within earshot of your message. You just don't know!

Twitter has unique advantages compared to texting. The ability to generate immediate—and frequent—publicity is one such advantage. This can be a positive or a negative for you, depending on the publicity generated.

Twitter can easily incorporate shortened Web URLs (links), though this is not a unique capability to Twitter. (Do note that a URL is much more likely to get clicked on by a recipient - a tweetee? - who's online on a computer; less so by a smartphone or PDA user.)

To use Twitter effectively, use it to augment other communications efforts, not to replace them. Avoid counting on a specific, given audience member being on Twitter. Even if you know they are on Twitter, do not count on them noticing a given tweet. If you think they will notice, do not count on them acting on it, even if it is just to click on a link.

Regard the tweet as the frosting on your communications cake - it's sweet, but it doesn't mean much without the rest of the cake there to support it.

Text-Style Email and More

The writing style used in texting affects all sorts of other communications. People send texts because of the brevity, clarity, and immediacy of the core foundation for texting communications – SMS text messages. They increasingly want the same, wherever possible, in other media.

Note that "wherever possible" only stretches so far. Many messages from corporate PR departments would be improved by being rendered as texts. "Gone With the Wind", "The Color Purple", or "Avatar" (all popular movies), not so much.

Before sending a text, think about whether the dynamics of some other platform, such as e-mail – or even a telephone call or hand-written note or letter – work better for your communications need. Also consider whether the clarity and brevity of text messages might usefully be carried over to the other medium.

In e-mail, the extreme form of abbreviation is to put the entire message in the header. This takes advantage of your e-mail note's reach and ubiquity to convey a quick message. The subject line might go something like this: "10am meeting delayed until 10:15am <ends>". This is texting by other means - in this case, via e-mail.

This strategy is especially worth considering given how e-mail is entrenched in society's communications model. More and more people have smartphones that are used for e-mail messaging. E-mail messages are still not as immediate and direct as text messages, but they're getting closer.

Many corporate presentations could benefit from a text-style make-over. Many presentation slides are crammed full of words. Yet communications experts recommend that a slide should have about 10 words or, better yet, a picture, with perhaps a word or two of description.

Text style can even be useful in that most personal of media, the in-person conversation. In the book, *The One-Minute Manager*, author Stephen Covey, recommends that conversations with employees begin with a compliment, contain a core message in the middle, then end on an upbeat note - all in a minute. A minute is time enough to say a couple of hundred words, maximum - or five or six texts' worth of communication.

We are inundated with messaging of one type or another. Learning, entertainment, fun, or meaningful time with someone important to you requires your uninterrupted attention. (And, hopefully, theirs.) To make time for these all-important, full-focus activities, it might be worth taking the lessons of texting into many of our other communications activities.

Txtversations: How Old Farts Must Communicate With Young Whipper-Snappers ...

Chapter 4. Better Txt

An entire genre of white papers, presentations and more exist on how to use texting for text message marketing. Marketing, as an in-depth topic, is not the focus of this book. I give note to text message marketing here briefly because it is an acknowledged use of texting as a messaging format. I then move on to the real focus of this book – how to use text messaging more effectively for day-to-day communications needs.

Text Message Marketing

Text message marketing is increasingly popular for individuals, politics, businesses, and other organizations. Yet my first thought about text message marketing is a take-off of a popular advertising slogan: just don't do it. My second thought is: if you <u>do</u> do it, do it very carefully.

Some of the great features of texting are seeming advantages for text message marketing: the way people keep their cell phones close to them; the immediacy and privacy of a text message; even the ability of a text message to wake you from a sound sleep.

Yet all of these features are minuses, as well - probably even more so - for marketing. Sales phone calls to home phones, often coming around dinnertime, so outraged the public that the national Do Not Call list was established to great effect. Text message marketing produces a similar response.

Many people still pay for each text message they receive. This is an acceptable arrangement when you receive a text message to tell you that the home heating repair visit that you scheduled has been bumped back a few hours. Less acceptable is receiving a text message advertisement for home heating repair from someone you never heard of.

What some deem more acceptable as a form of text message marketing are "useful" reminders and marketing notes that carry a strong information slant. For instance, if your university is trying to get students to apply, the admissions representative might ask people to sign up for text message updates about the application process.

This is marketing in the sense that it may increase the number of students who apply to your university, but it is information-based marketing. The message is meant to be perceived as a service by the students (and/or parents) who sign up.

A typical message in such a campaign might be: "Please sign up soon for college entrance exams for Fall 20XX admissions". You might even consider: "Narnia U Tops New Survey of Overseas Freshmen", if that indeed happened. You would definitely avoid "U Narnia rocks! Yeah!".

Some of these considerations apply to personal use of text messaging as well. Getting a friend to help you with your application for employment is one thing. Bombarding a recruiter with questions and unwanted information about yourself around the clock is another.

If you do consider text message marketing, first test it with people who are familiar with you. Map out your entire campaign, including your goals, both positive (get so many sales) and negative (avoiding more than a certain number of complaints). Proceed with caution. Infuriated former customers tend to tell a lot more people how they feel about you than satisfied current customers do.

Text-Speak and Text Message Abbreviations

Text-speak generally refers to the entire genre of communications via SMS text and similar message formats, as described in this book. We sometimes use the term "text-speak" to refer specifically to acronyms used in text messaging. These are more properly called Text Message Abbreviations - which you could refer to as TMAs, if you really wanted to take things to an extreme. (Perhaps this is "Too Much Abbreviation"?)

> "One of the basic tenets of communicating in a professional environment is demonstrating your command of the language."
>
> *– Sylvia Henderson*

Online dictionaries of text messaging abbreviations sometimes run to more than 1,000 entries! This is far more than most people can be expected to remember - or to figure out in context. Indeed, knowing a specific set of text messaging abbreviations shows that one is "in the know" in a specific "in group".

For your edification (and translation requirements), I present you with a few groups of text message abbreviations: a few everyone should know, and some others useful for specific groups.

How to Research TMAs

If you encounter an abbreviation with which you are unfamiliar, first try to figure it out from the overall context of the message. If you still need translation help, do a Web search using the words "text message" and the abbreviation itself (all without quotation marks). You should quickly find an answer.

Widely used general abbreviations follow. The first list specifically excludes abbreviations about laughing, grinning, and so on, which are in a separate list following. There are a lot of abbreviations, even in this shortened list; but if you look closely, you'll recognize many of them from other spheres of life or from your own texting experiences.

...More Effectively, & Vice Versa (So We Can Get On With Life & Get Things Accomplished)

Text Message Abbreviations: A Partial List

Abbreviation	Meaning
ASAP	As soon as possible
BTDT	Been there, done that. Sometimes added: "got the T-shirt" (GTTS).
BTW	By the way
CU, CUL	See you, See you later
C-YA!	See ya
EOM	End of message
F2F	Face to face, or in-person
FAQ	Frequently-ask question(s)
FUBAR	F***ed up beyond all repair (or recognition). Consider this an obscenity-based phrase. It is so common that I include it for your awareness.
FUD	Fear, Uncertainty, and Doubt
FYI	For your information
GIGO	Garbage in, garbage out. A technical description that has broad meaning in other spheres of life.
GMAB	Give me a break
IAW	I agree with, In accordance with
IHA	I hate acronyms. Ironically meant, of course!
IMHO	In my humble opinion
K	Okay
KISS	Keep it simple, stupid (or silly)
L8R	Later
NP or N/P	No problem

OIC	Oh, I see
OMG	Oh My God (or Gosh)
OTOH	On the other hand
RSN	Real soon now
RTFM	Read the f***ing manual. Again, consider this a frequently-used obscenity-based phrase.
S^	S'up - what's up
SNAFU	Situation normal, all f***ed up. This one started as WWII military jargon. Another obscenity-based phrase.
SOL	Sh*t out of luck. Yes, another obscenity-based phrase.
STW	Search the Web
SWAG	Stupid wild-a** guess, also known as scientific wild-a** guess
TAFN	That's all for now (alternative is TTFN, which stands for "ta-ta for now")
TGIF	Thank God (or gosh) it's Friday
THX	Thanks
TIA	Thanks in advance. Used as a "softener" at the end of a question or request.
TMA	Text message abbreviation.
TMI	Too much information.
TPTB	The powers that be. Refers to bosses, people who run a given Web site, and other "power people".
WTF	What the f***! This obscenity-based phrase is so common that I've seen it in the title of an article on a popular online site.

WYSIWYG	What you see is what you get. This originated with the publishing industry to indicate that what you type into a word processor and view on a screen is what you get when you print the document on your printer.
YW	You're welcome

Many text messaging abbreviations refer to laughing and/or crying. These references are so common that they are worth including in their own listing.

Abbreviation	Meaning
BEG	Big evil grin
BG	Big grin
BL	Belly laughing
BMGWL	Busting my gut with laughter
EG	Evil grin
FOMCL	Falling off my chair laughing
GD&R	Grinning, ducking, and running. Often added after a particularly sarcastic or inflammatory remark
LHO	Laughing *(implied "my")* head off
LMSO	Laughing my socks off; other LMO acronyms contain various obscenities in place of "socks"
LOL	Laughing out loud
ROTFL	Rolling on the floor, laughing

These lists are just a subset of the vast possibilities of text-message abbreviations. Texters frequently invent their own acronyms on the fly – usually variations on the above. Don't be afraid to try doing so yourself.

When you follow the conventions of a particular communications model, such as the TMAs listed here, you become more in-tune with, and accepted within, the circles of people who use said communications model. You also are better able to communicate with and understand messages from those who use the model, which is the whole point of this book!

Emoticons

The word "emoticon" is a clever combination of "emotional" and "icon", or symbol. The term represents a combination of keyboard characters that, together, make up something sort of recognizable as a face. Emoticons are a fun addition to txtversations, but should only be used in a personal, not a professional, context. (Occasionally, a smiley face, as described in the next paragraph, can help soften a professional message that might otherwise seem too direct.)

The original emoticon is :-), or just :), either of which is often automatically translated by messaging or word processing software to an actual smiley face symbol: ☺. (Writers, who occasionally come up with reasons to put a colon next to a close-parenthesis, are driven crazy by this auto-correction feature.)

In the "olden days" before word processing graphics were common features, the text generated by typewriter keyboards was the only means most people had to generate symbols akin to graphic characters. Much time and energy (as well as creativity) was spent devising text-character combinations to symbolize entire drawings. Some would say much of the same was wasted, but I digress.

The "smiley face" icon was derived from the original smiley face symbol, a very simple graphic usually rendered in black on yellow, often accompanied by the word, "Smile!"

There are many variations on the smiley face, which differ in several important ways:

- How widely they are recognized without analysis
- How easily they can be puzzled out if you think about it
- How likely they are to be translated to more easily recognizable symbols by various word-processing software. (Such translation may or may not be supported on the receiving end of the message.)

Good texting etiquette incorporates these emoticons where it "makes sense", but only where you are fairly sure that the recipient already knows the symbol as is, or can puzzle out your meaning. Otherwise, the recipient loses the meaning of the emoticon - which was often intended to lighten a harsh-sounding text message or invert its meaning completely. When your message recipient misinterprets your overall message, he or she is likely to be annoyed with you for causing them to feel ignorant for not knowing the meaning of the emoticon.

Professional use caution here: limit your use of emoticons in professional communications. An occasional smiley face never hurt anyone, and other people will probably use them with you at work. Yet err on the light use side in professional settings. I know…ironically, professional communications could use more humor!

One of the basic tenets of communicating in a professional environment is demonstrating your command of the language. When you use symbols (emoticons) or obscenities you demonstrate what is perceived in a professional context as an inability to use appropriate words that convey your intended message.

I remember my parents' admonition when I was a child that if I used curse words I was showing my ignorance of the beauty of language. That admonition has stuck with me to this day. Perception is reality for most of us. Using emoticons in professional communications implies that you cannot – or refuse to – frame your message to reduce the chance that your message receiver misinterprets your meaning.

For personal use, if you know the other party uses the same type of phone or instant messaging software as you use, and your software translates an emoticon to an understandable graphic symbol, then you have a wider palette from which to draw. In the interest of supporting the broadest possible communications understanding, I deliberately keep the following list of emoticons to a short list with which I recommend you become familiar in order to effectively communicate in a texting context.

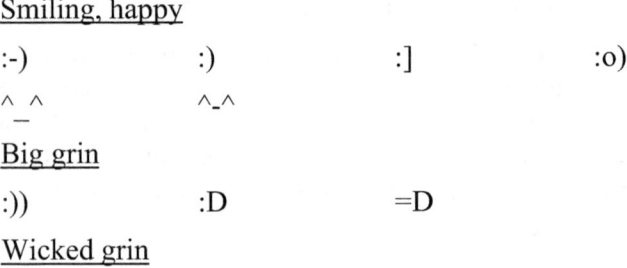

Smiling, happy

:-)   :)   :]   :o)

^_^   ^-^

Big grin

:))   :D   =D

Wicked grin

:>   =>   :o/

Sad

:-(:o(:[:<

Shocked or surprised

:o   =o   :(]

o-o (and variations with an "o" on either end and another character between)

Tongue in cheek

:P   :-P   =P   :9

Others

;) and others with a semicolon instead of a colon - wink

:□ Bored, annoyed

:S Confused, embarrassed, uneasy

Txtversations: How Old Farts <u>Must</u> Communicate With Young Whipper-Snappers ...

Chapter 5. Txt Mastery

Mastering text messaging is a challenge, but one you can meet. I recommend that you take some time, over the next few weeks, to consider how you're using texting; to help it find the right place in your communications repertoire; and to test out different uses of texting with various types of people. Over time, texting will become comfortable, at which point you can congratulate yourself. You will have achieved text mastery!

This chapter offers suggestions and guidelines. It is difficult to provide hard and fast rules for texting. As in any form of human communications, it's a bit like the scene starring Brad Pitt in the movie *Fight Club*: "The first rule of fight club is - there are no rules!"

While this absence of absolute rules is true for texting as well, there are a few things I can help you think about before you press Send on a long, detailed, angry text to your boss, who's attending a conference in a city where it's 3am, when she or he has a breakfast meeting at 7am.

Fixing Common Texting Errors

This chapter presents common texting errors that cut across the texts you might send, or not send, and their remedies.

1. Stay in others' comfort zone

When you speak to someone, you can see their reaction. When you text them, you can't. So it is easy to overdo it when texting someone. If you are not getting much feedback, reduce your texts to them to a similar level to their texts to you. Avoid wearing out your textual welcome.

2. Stay in your own comfort zone

You might be texting so much that you hurt yourself. Texting, typing, and otherwise (over)using fine motor skills can wear out your hands, sometimes leading to serious repetitive injury. If you're experiencing minor pain or occasional numbness, find a phone that is very comfortable for you to use and reduce your texting. If it gets worse, see a doctor, as these problems can become quite serious.

3. Keep it even shorter than you have to

While 160 characters is the mechanical maximum, at about 25 words, 160 characters is a really long text message. One sentence of 8-10 words, less than half the maximum, is as much as most experienced texters expect to get. Even if you're texting from a computer, try to keep your texts to this length.

4. Keep on texting

I have heard people get really angry at receiving a voice mail message - or not getting information at all - when a text would have been a quick, easy solution. This is a case of knowing your audience, as other people find texts annoying. If someone texts you regularly, consider using text messaging when you have a brief message for them.

5. Keep a bit of distance

Getting texts that are too familiar - too many virtual winks, hugs, and kisses, whether through words, text message abbreviations, or emoticons (see the previous chapter) - can be anywhere from cute, to funny, to creepy. As with the number of texts you exchange, match the tone of the texts you send to the tone of the texts you receive from each of your correspondents. In professional settings, complete sentences (short and concise, please) are most appropriate.

6. Eschew obscenities

Among friends, the occasional rude word can be very much on point, or even very, very funny. Crude language, however, is seldom the right approach. While I dislike using the word "never", when your image is at stake and you want your image to be a positive one, crude language is never the approach to take. Always remember that texts can be forwarded, and instant messages can remain in the "web-isphere" for a long, long time. Consider photos of body parts usually kept covered as completely inappropriate to distribute.

7. Avoid sloppiness

Our tolerance for misspellings ranges from absolute annoyance to bemused acceptance to positive appreciation. (Some people feel misspellings in text messages are friendly.) Abbreviation is almost always acceptable (though "u" for "you" feels quite familiar); out and out errors, not so much.

8. Use informality

If you want to appear to Not Get It - to be completely out of tune with the times - just send texts with formal wording, proper spelling and full punctuation to most texters. The exception: communications for professional purposes.

9. Support interaction

If a topic requires interaction or nuance, texting usually just doesn't cut it. One example of such a situation is negotiating terms and conditions of a contract. Such negotiations involve communications far more appropriate for in-person or telephone interaction, where voice and physical appearance add to the messages. An appropriate time to text in negotiations, however, might be at the end when you send, "All OK. Sign the contract!"

10. Send the right message

Some messages are not text-friendly. Even hinting that you're breaking up with someone, or about to fire them, is a major text faux pas; actually doing either of these by text will get you bad press or bad feelings about you.

Whom You Text

When new technologies come along, they often disrupt traditional patterns of communications. When email first became popular, many people believed hierarchies in organizations would just about disappear! However, over time, traditional models tend to adapt to fit new technology, rather than just disappearing.

Differences in job role, age, even social position, and how well you know someone, can affect how you should handle texting them, or responding to a text from them. Often, it's uncomfortable to text someone you don't know well, but necessary.

Here are a few guidelines to consider when you decide with whom you should text:

- **Avoid overusing a mobile phone number.** You may only have a work colleague's phone number because it is on a list for work emergencies. You also may not know if they have a text message plan. Avoid using that number for a text message unless you have an urgent need. Keep your message brief and on point.
- **Be polite**. Strive to avoid being over familiar. Be polite and brief.
- **Keep from demanding a response**. If you feel uncomfortable texting someone, but think that you need to anyway, don't demand a response. Just provide needed information. The person will usually send a brief "thanks" to acknowledge receipt.
- **Use multiple channels**. Use a text message as an alert; use email or the phone for details, or refer someone to a third party who has the needed information.

Conversely, work over time to develop a friendly, conversational texting tone with people you know well. You can develop your own vocabulary - a few appropriate text message abbreviations, an emoticon or two - to use for casual txtversations.

Why You Text

Communications depend heavily on context. However, the only context your receiver has access to is the general, overall context of your message. They have no way of knowing if you are upset, worried, anxious, or angry from how you look and your tone of voice.

Use these suggestions to have your text message appropriately reflect the reasons you're sending a text message:

- **Don't inflict urgency on people via text message**. The recipient may be in a completely different mental or emotional space from you. A text from an anxious work colleague - or, worse, boss - can completely disrupt someone's work, their meeting, or, if they are home, important "quality time" with a significant other.

- **Do keep negative emotions to yourself**. Avoid being terse, sarcastic, sardonic, or especially angry. (Sometimes even friendly text messages can seem to be some of these things, just because of the medium; if you really are upset, it may come across tenfold.) Remember, too, that it's easy for the victim of any outbursts of yours to forward or show the text around, making you look like a jerk.

- **Don't confess your love**. If you like someone more than they know, tell them in person, or at least on the phone - don't try to shoehorn such important news into the narrow emotional bandwidth of a text message. Not only are these other media richer and more powerful, to better serve your purpose; if you misjudge the situation, what you say can be laughed off later, whereas what you text can stay around for a looooong time.

- **Do affirm your love**. Once someone does know you love them, a text message can be a great reminder. Just don't make them blush when they're in an important meeting.

When You Text

Thinking about the timing of a text is a close cousin to thinking about the tone. You need to think not only about where someone is - physically and emotionally – but also what time it is for the other person, both the actual time and what time it might *feel* like to them at the moment.

In your same time zone, this can mean accounting for the cycle of someone else's day. Just because you finished school at 3pm does not mean your Mom or Dad is off work and ready to read all about your day in a text. Use a text message to ask them to call you, rather than to fill in all the ups and down. Similarly for someone lucky enough to be able to sleep in later than you do. 8am is pretty early for some people!

Bedtimes can be tricky, too. Being awakened by a text is really, really annoying. Impose a severe curfew on yourself. Many people prefer not to receive a call or a text after 9pm or so. However, others literally go to bed with their phones in hand, napping in between text exchanges and phone calls long into the night. Assume someone is a 9pm-er until you know better.

Drive time is also no time to text. Never text when you drive. Doing so is extremely distracting and dangerous. Trying to find the right key, or read the tiny little onscreen characters, takes your attention off the road.

Also, try to avoid texting someone else when they are driving. (You cannot always know, but sometimes you can make a pretty good guess.) It is just too tempting for someone to check, just in case the meeting's been cancelled or a child has come down with the flu.

The time when it's really easy to mess up is when someone is in a different time zone than you are. It's not enough just to avoid the obvious, but all too easy to make, mistake of calling or texting in the middle of the night. People who are jet-lagged often sleep a) at odd hours and b) poorly, and need to be left alone whenever they do manage to catch forty winks.

Don't assume a text is a huge improvement over a call, either. Texts have to be read. For me, that means finding my reading glasses, perhaps flipping on a light, and, worse, focusing my brain into reading mode. It's almost easier to fumble for a ringing phone in the dark, growl at someone to leave me alone, then get back to sleep.

Yet texts are a vital, relatively inexpensive method of communication with someone who's travelling, often the only affordable and reliable alternative. Minimize your texts, and try to stay within agreed upon hours, so the traveller has a known break - from you, if not from everyone else who might try to get in touch.

When To Avoid Texting

Let's be honest: texting is a great way to be in touch with someone with whom you should not be in touch. You can send secret little love messages back and forth without being overheard speaking in your sappiest, lovey-dovey voice, at times of your convenience, all with the thrill of doing something you shouldn't.

However, every text message you send and receive shows up on your phone bill, along with the number used - and, often most incriminating, the time of day. (It's a rare tennis coach or work colleague who texts you at 7am, 3pm, 7pm, and 3am as well.)

Texts are stored on your phone, easily read by anyone who gets hold of it - which can happen at the most inopportune times. And, do you really think that little smirk you get when you read a text message from that special, secret someone can be explained away as your delight at finding out that bananas are on special today at the market?

Texts can be used as conclusive evidence in a way phone records are not. The times of phone calls might *imply* something is going on; only the contents of the texts you sent and received *prove* it.

As the saying goes, hell hath no fury like a woman - or a man - scorned. Don't send or receive a text that would really cause you trouble if it were put up in lights in Times Square. That's the only way to truly stay safe.

Txtversations: How Old Farts <u>Must</u> Communicate With Young Whipper-Snappers ...

...More Effectively, & Vice Versa (So We Can Get On With Life & Get Things Accomplished)

Chapter 6. Txtversations

This book addresses the basics of using text messaging - the technology, the different ways people use it, mistakes that people make, and tools for getting more out of it.

Texting continues to increase in popularity. "Get on the train or die" is an old saying used in technology when a new approach or tool becomes so useful that you can no longer ignore it. This is a harsh way of saying that you can only fool around with - or ignore - a tool for so long. Eventually, you have to jump on board. For most of us, texting is at that point.

Now it's time for strategy. How can you use texting - not just individual text messages, but complete txtversations - to better accomplish your goals in life? This chapter will give you some ideas.

Txtversational Green, Yellow, and Red Light Zones

You practically <u>have</u> to use texting some of the time these days. Certain communications can best be achieved by texting. If you are over 40, as I may or may not be (ahem), you will have to trust me on this: few people younger than you want to receive voice mail messages from you. Send a text or an e-mail message instead.

In situations where only a text will do, you'll fail at basic communications tasks if you use some other medium instead.

More subtly, if texting is the best thing to do for a given communications need, with a given person, then not texting when you "should" will cause the other person aggravation and frustration.

However, you may also be a too-frequent texter, especially if you were born and grew up entirely during the "age of cell phones". You may have regular "correspondents" with whom you've been exchanging texts for years. Every new text sent to or received from that person adds to a rich conversation that's been going on for the entire time you've known them, and which also includes emails, Facebook updates, phone calls, time spent together, as well as txtversations and other kinds of conversations with mutual friends.

When communicating with people who are not as text-savvy as are you, you need to text less. These people think of conversations more as discrete occurrences, not as an ongoing stream - and they put great importance on mutual respect, appropriateness, and other subtle factors.

Older people also tend to segment their lives and their relationships more. They divide people rather neatly into friends, family, acquaintances, work colleagues, and so on. They try to divide their days up into clear-cut segments as well, and often feel that communications that break through these barriers are intrusive and unwelcome.

For a younger person to text an older person can feel disrespectful, in which case they'll be upset - or, it can feel inclusive, in which case they'll be pleased. (See: sons, daughters, grandchildren, above.) In situations where only a text will do, of course, you need to send a text. But if another communications medium will do the job, consider using that instead.

To sum up: those who are less experienced with texting need to learn to text competently. Those who spend a great deal of time sending casual texts need to learn to text professionally.

Green-light zones for texting

Texting is great for brief alerts, little bits of information that the other person can take in and, if needed, acknowledge. Here are a few examples:

- <u>Family member at home</u>: "**Please pick up some eggs on the way home**".
- <u>Family member out of the house</u>: "**OK**" or "**sure**". (Or, informally: "**k**".)

This tiny exchange is fraught with possibilities for warmth or rudeness, relationship-building or the perception of disrespect. For instance, receiving the response of "k" instead of "OK" would feel intimate and warm to some, rude and disrespectful to others. Older people in particular will count every character in a response and feel that the other party is being lazy or downright rude if they send too few.

Few young people would request eggs by sending a full English sentence. "Pls bring home eggs" might be the most you should hope for. (If you are younger, please include that "pls". Politeness makes life so much easier, in text as elsewhere.)

Other green-light type text messages - which younger people would tend to shorten considerably:

- "**Your plane will be 40 minutes late**"
- "**The Board meeting is postponed 30 minutes**"
- "**Our stock just went up 10 points**" (or: "**OURCO +10 NYSE**")

- **"Meeting starts in 15 minutes - please have presentation with you"**.

Any brief hit of information which might be urgent or actionable, or a simple request - and which requires either no reply, or just an acknowledgement, not a substantive response - can and, usually, should be sent by text.

If you are an infrequent texter, discipline yourself to nearly always send this kind of "quick hit" message by text. It's cheap, easy, simple, and, these days, the expected thing to do. When used for a brief update, a text imposes much less hassle on the recipient than the (increasingly loathed) voice mail message.

If you are a too-frequent texter and looking to cut back - especially with people who don't get a lot of texts, and might consider them rude - continue to use texts for these kinds of simple, direct messages. It's the right thing to do, and people will appreciate it.

Red-light zones for texting

Text messaging should be avoided with some kinds of communications. These are messages that are unusual in some way:

- **Unusually important (good)**. Really important good news should, if possible, be shared in person, or at least by phone. Of course, if text is the only way, go for it. ("It's a girl!" is a fun kind of text to receive.)

- **Unusually important (bad)**. People are often tempted to send bad news by text because it seems so easy. "You're fired", "I'm running off to Texas with your best friend", and "Sorry, it *is* contagious" are all messages that seem easier to communicate via text. However, from that day on, ever-widening circles of people will think you're a creep. Treat the intense desire to send bad news as a text as a 100% reliable signal that you shouldn't do it.

- **Long, complicated, or subtle**. People quickly scan texts; they don't want to carefully read them. So avoid length, complexity, or irony. Instead, send an e-mail or make a phone call. (You can use texting to alert someone to the email or set up the phone call.)

- **Highly interactive**. Sometimes a short text message is like a string sticking out from a ball of yarn - soon, you've unraveled the whole thing in a long flurry of messages back and forth. For instance, ordering a meal can be like a game of twenty questions: "Chicken, beef, or tofu?" "Rare, medium, or well-done?" "Soup or salad?" "Still water, or sparkling?" Don't start something in text if you're sure to end up finishing it in email or on the phone.

- **Very personal**. If something is really personal, it is important, to at least one of the people involved. That means that if they have any questions or comments, they will be really annoyed to have to text them. Deliver very personal news in person if you can, by phone if you have to, but via text only if you truly must.

If you are an infrequent texter, beware of making these rookie errors. Build up your texting skills with green light texts, as discussed in the previous section; then, gradually move into yellow light texts, as described in the next section. Stay out of the red light district!

If you are a too-frequent texter, you are probably already spending time in the red light zone, sending deeply personal, important, or complicated messages by text. That's OK with people who enjoy doing the same. In the short term, be aware of what you do. Realize that texting about everything in your universe to people who text infrequently may prove unwelcome. Over time, look to cut back on red-light messages with just about all your contacts. The worthwhile things in life are too important to communicate with just a few texted words at a time!

Yellow-light zones for texting

The yellow light for texting is for text messages that many people will think appropriate. Other people will think otherwise.

This is, of course, a vague and confusing category. The best example of the yellow-light zone might come from Twitter. The introductory sentence for Twitter has justly become famous: "What are you doing?"

That, in itself, is a yellow-light message. Most older people would never send a text saying, "What are you doing?" This is an open-ended question that might require a long, complicated answer. Most older people would call with a question like that.

Younger people are entirely comfortable with this kind of message. In fact, for younger people who text a lot, the question "What are you doing?" is always hanging out there. Younger people continually answer that question through their texts to each other.

Yellow-light messages are generally appropriate with peers: Good friends, romantic partners, work colleagues who like texting about as much (or as little) as you do. Usually, they work best in the same age range - maybe as much as ten years on either side of your own age.

If you are an infrequent texter, build up your text messaging with a couple of selected people, and see if you're both comfortable in this yellow-light zone. It's a fun place to spend time, and can enrich a friendship, work relationship, or romantic relationship. Perhaps you'll even end up with someone you can occasionally visit the red-light zone with!

If you are a frequent texter, don't assume that others are comfortable in the yellow-light zone just because you are. When in doubt, pick up the phone or, if possible, speak in person.

Using Texting Style in Other Media

Texting is likely to increase as an acceptable and expected part of our overall communications mix. As the text-friendly "younger generations" move further into and up through the workforce, and the text-avoidant older generations move out, the texting use rules will also change in the professional environment.

The reasons people text more are also likely to increase: we are constantly bombarded with greater communications, more-complex media, and more data, often doing several things at once. Texts cut through the clutter - even as they add to it.

As texting and information overload do indeed increase, the text style of sending messages might also have an increasing effect on how people use other communications media. Here are some positive changes you might consider introducing across your communications mix:

+ **Shorter messages**. Many of us over 40 love to compose and send long e-mails. These may be increasingly unappreciated and even unread. Remember KISS: Keep It Short and Simple. You might also consider shortening voice mail messages (when you have to use them), conversational statements, presentations, and speeches.

+ **Wider use of TMAs and emoticons.** Text message abbreviations and emoticons, such as smiley faces, may become more common in email and other written communications. Good thing you have this book for reference, when you want to use them or understand them! Some email systems already have menus from which you can select emoticons as integral parts of writing notes.

+ **More self-contained messages.** Smartphones tend to preserve txtversations by keeping all your text messages with a given party together. Even so, you can easily lose the context of exchanges in text, e-mail, and voicemail messages. Consider keeping your messages not only brief but self-contained; send an alert, rather than the opening salvo in an exchange.

That is the good news; what negative text-based trends should you look out for, and avoid in your communications? Here are a few suggestions:

- **Terseness and rudeness.** To many older people, terseness and rudeness are almost the same thing. Avoid carrying a level of terseness that might be acceptable in text messages into other media, where it may be more likely to be interpreted as rude.

- **Obscenities, expressed or implied.** World War II caused several obscenity-based phrases such as "snafu" to enter common speech. (See Chapter 4 if these abbreviations are unfamiliar to you.) Texting is causing a whole new wave. I have even seen "WTF?", a widely known - and quite obscene - TMA, used in the headline of a mainstream blog. Avoid this! It will embarrass many people and leave others appalled - including you, if your boss has to ask you what WTF means in the middle of a big presentation!

- **Oh, the inhumanity.** We quoted Marshall McLuhan's famous saying, "the medium is the message", in Chapter 2. However, sometimes the message is the message. If you're firing someone, dumping them, or otherwise ruining someone's life, it's not enough to avoid doing it by text message. You also have to use words freely instead of sparingly, express sympathy or empathy, and otherwise be both human and humane about it.

Your Txtversational Style

All of us have a conversational style. New technologies often catch us off guard - and encourage us to try new approaches. To be effective in using text messaging, your txtversational style needs to become an extension of your style in other media.

Every day you communicate with people. In-person conversation is the most complex communication; it includes your appearance, your body language (even when you don't speak at all), your tone of voice, and the actual words you say.

Other forms of communication strip away this complexity, a layer at a time. A phone call takes away the visual element; e-mail takes away your tone of voice as a tool.

In texting, not only are you limited to only words; you're limited to very few of those. This shifts attention to other aspects of communications that usually don't get as much attention. Think about how you usually handle each of these elements, and how you should then handle them in txtversations.

Frequency

Texting breaks the frequency of communications down to a very basic level. Every text you send and receive is recorded on your phone bill. (Which is not always a good thing, as we mentioned in the previous chapter.) If you're not on a plan, or you are beyond the plan's limits - perhaps, for instance, when texting internationally - every text you send costs you money as well.

Texting also makes it painfully clear who is starting an exchange and who's responding. There's no way to talk over each other in text, or for one person to send a non-verbal signal, such as walking in a room and smiling at you, to which you might respond verbally. Each act of sending and receiving a text message is considered, separate, and independent.

How frequently do you communicate with different people? And, how frequently do you start a conversation? How frequently does the other person start a conversation with you?

The temptation, with texting, is to use texting's ease of use and lack of social cues to break down social barriers; to communicate with more people, more frequently, than we would do otherwise. This is a bad idea in the long run; it can make people annoyed with you or, even worse, it can make them dismissive of your attempts to communicate.

We have all probably heard someone say, when their phone rings or a text arrives, "Oh, it's *him* (or *her*) again." No one wants to be that "him" or "her"!

If you are usually the one who initiates a conversation with a given person, you may need to continue doing so when you text that person, or needed exchanges will never take place.

But in txtversations, you do not have body language, tone of voice, or even the use of a lot of words to tip you off if you are over-communicating.

Until you find a formula for txtversations with someone with which you are sure you are both comfortable, keep your texting frequency to a minimum. To establish a comfort level, watch responses carefully – not just direct responses in text, but how the person refers to your texting them in other communications.

Responsiveness

The flip side of sending a text is the response you get back - if any. I have heard complaints from friends who have texted someone and not heard back. How quickly you respond, or even whether you respond at all, is a critical part of txtversations.

I recommend that you do your best to respond to texts, if only with an acknowledgement. Earlier in this chapter I recommended that you use "alert"-style texts where possible, which are messages that are complete and self-contained. When you receive such a message, a brief acknowledgement is usually welcome. "Thx" is good, but can seem cold as a text message; with someone with whom you are friendly, "Thank you!" may be better. (And yes, you should take the time to capitalize the "T", if your texting software doesn't do it for you.)

How quickly to respond? Generally, right away is best. An unanswered text can generate any or all of: anxiety on the sender's part; a follow-up text; an e-mail; a phone call; or a stroll by your desk. If someone knows you have the habit of responding quickly, they will worry less, even when you don't.

There are, of course, exceptions. Many "yellow light" texts can wait. If someone texts "How RU doing?", you might wait until you're actually doing something interesting to respond. Of course, then you might risk offending the person with whom you are doing something interesting!

Content and Tone

The words of text messages, even whether the words are spelled out or not, can be parsed, character by character, to discern the tone which the sender meant to communicate in their text. Text messages tend to sound cold and dismissive. On the other hand, attempts to warm them up - such as the concluding exclamation point in "Thanks!" - can seem silly or even fake.

With people unfamiliar to you, it is probably better to risk seeming a bit silly (which could be embarrassing for you) than to risk seeming a bit cold (which could be embarrassing, or even hurtful, for them). If you become text buddies, you can become more casual over time.

The Rules

Breaking the rules of any kind of communication is the source of much offense - and also of much humor and fun. We mentioned before that the very occasional, exceedingly well-placed obscenity can be hilarious. Similarly with other rules.

Being informal with a boss can communicate that you're comfortable with him and her. Not bothering to fix a misspelling can imply friendliness rather than illiteracy. And so on.

The people who get the most respect in any communications medium are those who repeatedly demonstrate that they know what the rules are and how to follow them, and then break them, occasionally and appropriately. "Appropriately", of course, means different things to different people, which is part of the fun.

Txtversations: How Old Farts <u>Must</u> Communicate With Young Whipper-Snappers ...

So What? Now What?

Great! You now know about how text messaging evolved and have some guidelines on when to text and when not to. You have a quick reference to start you out on your texting skills practice and to help you understand what others are "saying" when they text. So what? Now what do you do with this information?

It's valuable to be seen as a competent communicator, and your comfort level with technology like texting reflects strongly on how your competence is perceived.

You want to be seen as someone who uses texts well; who avoids giving offense; who gets the message across; who reassures, or even inspires, right along with providing information.

You can use texting to convey familiarity and friendship, thus building up a relationship - or, by reducing your interactions with someone and conducting more of the interactions via text, to phase one out.

Look at your important relationships through the lens of texting. Where can you use text to get routine tasks done, to save "face time" for the important relationship interactions in your life? Before you press "send", ask yourself whether your message is one that is better conveyed some other way.

Are you a frequent and comfortable texter? Use what you read in this book to better communicate with and understand those for whom texting is not yet a communications norm.

Are you a text-avoider or unfamiliar with texting as your primary communications tool? Then use what you read in these pages to get with the program and get texting. If you have any hope for staying in tune and in touch with those who will make decisions about your future and your business some day very soon, you must learn to communicate effectively on their terms.

These are basic, effective communications principles. Your image; your results; your success depends on them!

About the Author

Sylvia Henderson runs a business called Springboard Training. She helps people show they are as great as they say they are. She facilitates workshops and conference general sessions, keynotes, develops educational tools, and authors books and program-related articles.

She works with individuals and organizations (businesses, associations, non-profits, educational, and government) to make their "people image" (interpersonal skills) match - or exceed - their organizational image for greater profit, more clients, and a higher degree of personal and professional success.

Sylvia integrates principles of adult learning into her programs by actively engaging audiences in the learning process, using toys and props to generate interest and emphasize points. She weaves her avocation as a motorcyclist into analogies and metaphors that tie into messages targeting your needs.

Sylvia's real-world experiences include 20+ years as a corporate trainer, team leader and manager practicing the leadership, communication and motivational skills she now presents in her programs. She serves on nonprofit Boards of Directors and is Past-President of both national and professional non-profit associations.

Sign up for monthly content, download resources you can use immediately, and bring Sylvia to your organization at www.springboardtraining.com – contact us. Blog: http://blog.springboardtraining.com. Twitter: @SuccessLanguage.

Txtversations: How Old Farts <u>Must</u> Communicate With Young Whipper-Snappers ...

www.ingramcontent.com/pod-product-compliance
Lightning Source LLC
LaVergne TN
LVHW051848080426
835512LV00018B/3143